GREAT MINECRAFT® BUILDS

YOUR UNOFFICIAL GUIDE TO

BUILDING COOL MINECRAFT® CASTLES

S. D. MORISON

Enslow PUBLISHING

Please visit our website, www.enslow.com. For a free color catalog of all our high-quality books, call toll free 1-800-398-2504 or fax 1-877-980-4454.

Cataloging-in-Publication Data
Names: Morison, S. D.
Title: Your unofficial guide to building cool Minecraft® castles / S. D. Morison.
Description: New York : Enslow Publishing, 2023. | Series: Great Minecraft® builds | Includes glossary and index.
Identifiers: ISBN 9781978529267 (pbk.) | ISBN 9781978529281 (library bound) | ISBN 9781978529274 (6pack) | ISBN 9781978529298 (ebook)
Subjects: LCSH: Minecraft (Game)–Juvenile literature. | Castles–Computer simulation–Juvenile literature. | Castles–Design and construction–Juvenile literature.
Classification: LCC GV1469.35.M535 M672 2023 | DDC 794.8–dc23

Published in 2023 by
Enslow Publishing
29 E. 21st Street
New York, NY 10010

Portions of this work were originally authored by Jill Keppeler and published as *The Unofficial Guide to Building Castles in Minecraft*. All new material this edition authored by S. D. Morison.

Designer: Rachel Rising
Editor: Jill Keppeler
Illustrator: Matías Lapegüe

Photo credits: Cover, pp. 1-4, 6, 8, 10, 12, 14, 16, 18, 20, 22-24 Orange Sky ART/Shutterstock.com; Cover, pp. 1-24 Phoenix 1319/ Shutterstock.com; Cover, pp. 1, 3, 6, 8, 10, 12, 16, 22-24 Soloma/Shutterstock.com; p. 4 Matt Gibson/Shutterstock.com; pp. 6, 8, 10, 12, 16 Phoenix 1319/Shutterstock.com; p. 7 leoks/Shutterstock.com; p. 11 slawjanek_fotografia/Shutterstock.com; p. 14 Valery Egorov/ Shutterstock.com; p. 17 Karen Foster/Shutterstock.com; p. 18 donsimon/Shutterstock.com.

Printed in the United States of America

CPSIA compliance information: Batch #CSENS23: For further information contact Enslow Publishing, New York, New York, at 1-800-398-2504.

CONTENTS

Words in the glossary appear in **bold** type the first time they are used in the text.

BEST BUILDS EVER

There are many possibilities for buildings in both the real world and the world of *Minecraft*. People **design** and build houses, businesses, schools, and more. However, perhaps the coolest type of building in either world is a castle! Tough and towering, **protective** and powerful, castles served as a safe space for people in earlier times.

In *Minecraft*, castles can serve as a home base. They can be a safe space to get through the dark, monster-filled night or to store your supplies and building **materials**. You can be as **creative** as you want!

A *Minecraft* castle can start small. Maybe build a tower to start!

Materials:

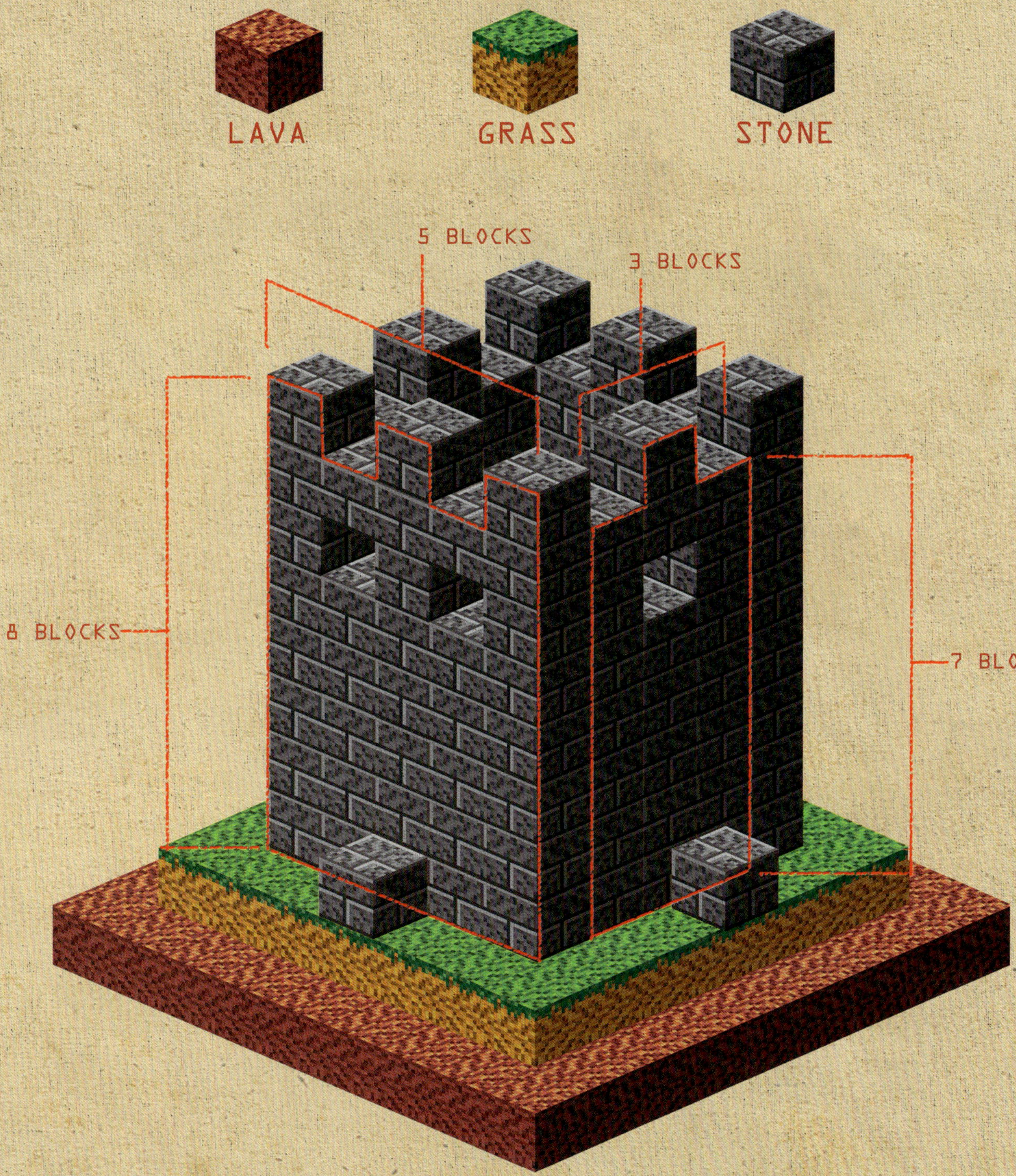

THE HISTORY OF CASTLES

Throughout history, people have built castles all over the world—in Africa, India, and Japan, as well as other locations. However, most castles were built in Europe during the time called Middle Ages, which took place from about 500 to 1500 CE. They were home to kings, lords, and their people. However, unlike palaces, castles were **fortified** and had many **defenses**.

People built early castles out of dirt and wood. Later, they began to use stone, which is how we usually think of castles today. Dirt, wood, and stone are all common materials in *Minecraft*!

ADVENTURE MODE

Sometimes people decide to copy historic castles in *Minecraft*. They can be enormous builds!

What parts of historic castles can you copy *Minecraft*? You can put lots of parts togethe

DIFFERENT RULES

One cool thing about building in *Minecraft* is that some of the natural rules are different from those in the real world. For example, most blocks aren't affected by **gravity**! You don't have to worry about a huge block or slab of stone falling on you or crushing your build.

People used to use arches and other shapes when building castles because they could support a lot of weight. You don't have to worry about that in *Minecraft*, but arches can still be a cool way to add **detail** to a build.

ADVENTURE MODE

Some *Minecraft* blocks are affected by gravity. These include gravel, sand, and concrete powder. They'll fall if there's no support underneath them!

Stone bricks can be a good material for a *Minecraft* castle build. Bake cobblestone blocks in a furnace, then combine four stone blocks to make four stone brick blocks.

WHERE TO BUILD

In the real world, people built many castles at the sides of mountains or hills. Their walls might surround many other buildings, including stables and blacksmith workshops. If you want to have something similar in *Minecraft*, you can build your castle walls around a nonplayer character (NPC) village.

You might have to chop down a lot of trees to clear space for your castle. When things are clear enough, mark off the space you want surrounded by castle walls. Use math to figure out how many building materials you'll need.

ADVENTURE MODE

***Minecraft* NPC villages have different types of buildings depending on where they're found. For example, buildings in desert villages are often made of sandstone.**

If you don't want to build your castle around an NPC village, you'll have more **flexibility** on location. And you can design your own buildings!

CASTLE CONCERNS

There are other things to keep in mind for your castle. While the earliest real-world castles had a wooden main building, wood isn't as strong as stone—either in the real world or in *Minecraft*. It can catch fire and burn down. In *Minecraft*, it doesn't have high blast resistance. This is how well a material will stand up to an **explosion**.

You also need to be sure you can keep all the spaces inside your castle walls well lit. If it's too dark, monsters such as zombies and creepers will **spawn** there!

ADVENTURE MODE

Explosions in *Minecraft* can be caused by creepers, TNT, destroyed end crystals, and a few other things.

Stone keep castles were stronger than the early wooden forts and castles. This is true in *Minecraft* too!

UP HIGH, DOWN LOW

Castle walls and buildings often have tall towers. If you build stairs in a tower or add a ladder to climb up to the top, you can see all around. You'll know if dangerous monsters or other players are approaching. If you have a bow or crossbow and arrows, you can fire on enemies!

Castle walls can be one or many blocks wide. The wider the wall, the harder it will be for something—an enemy or an explosion—to break through it! If you make wider walls, you can also walk along them.

Castle towers can be square or round. You can't make real circles in *Minecraft*, but you can get close.

IN THE CASTLE KEEP

A keep was the main structure inside castle walls. It was the safest, strongest part, built of stone and containing living and storage space. This is what many people think of as the castle itself. It might have its own towers and extra walls. Anything valuable would be kept there.

A keep might have its own huge dining hall. It would have its own well so people could get water if they were stuck there during a **siege**. There might also be decorations like stained-glass windows!

ADVENTURE MODE

You can make stained glass in *Minecraft*. Bake sand in a furnace to make glass, then add dye from flowers or other sources.

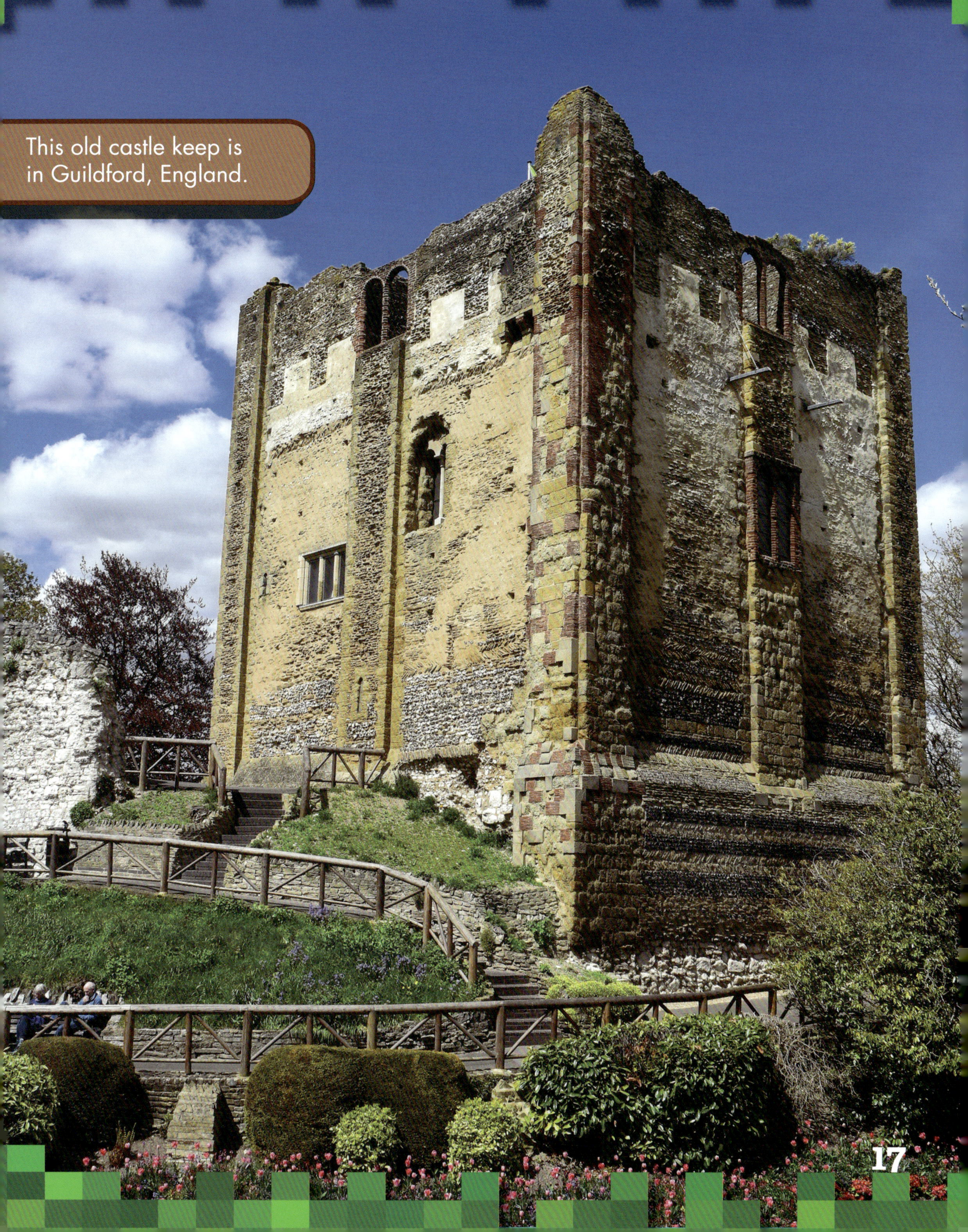

This old castle keep is in Guildford, England.

THE WAYS OF WATER

Water doesn't work the same way in *Minecraft* as it does in the real world. You can place a water source using a bucket full of water, but it only spreads so much from side to side. A waterfall in *Minecraft*, however, will fall downward as long as there's space!

Many real-life castles had moats—channels full of water—around them. You can make a moat in *Minecraft*, but you might have to experiment a bit because of the differences. Empty a bucket of water onto every block surface within your moat and go from there.

People could lower bridges over a moat to let others into a castle—and raise them to keep enemies out.

FANTASY AND REALITY

You can make a *Minecraft* castle that's realistic in many ways. You can use sturdy stone walls, a moat, and a castle keep to protect your supplies and treasures. You can copy a historic castle or design one all your own.

But you don't need to stay realistic! You can also make a fantasy castle if you want to. You can use materials like gold and emerald blocks, or even ice and snow. This kind of castle might not be as tough, but it can be very creative!

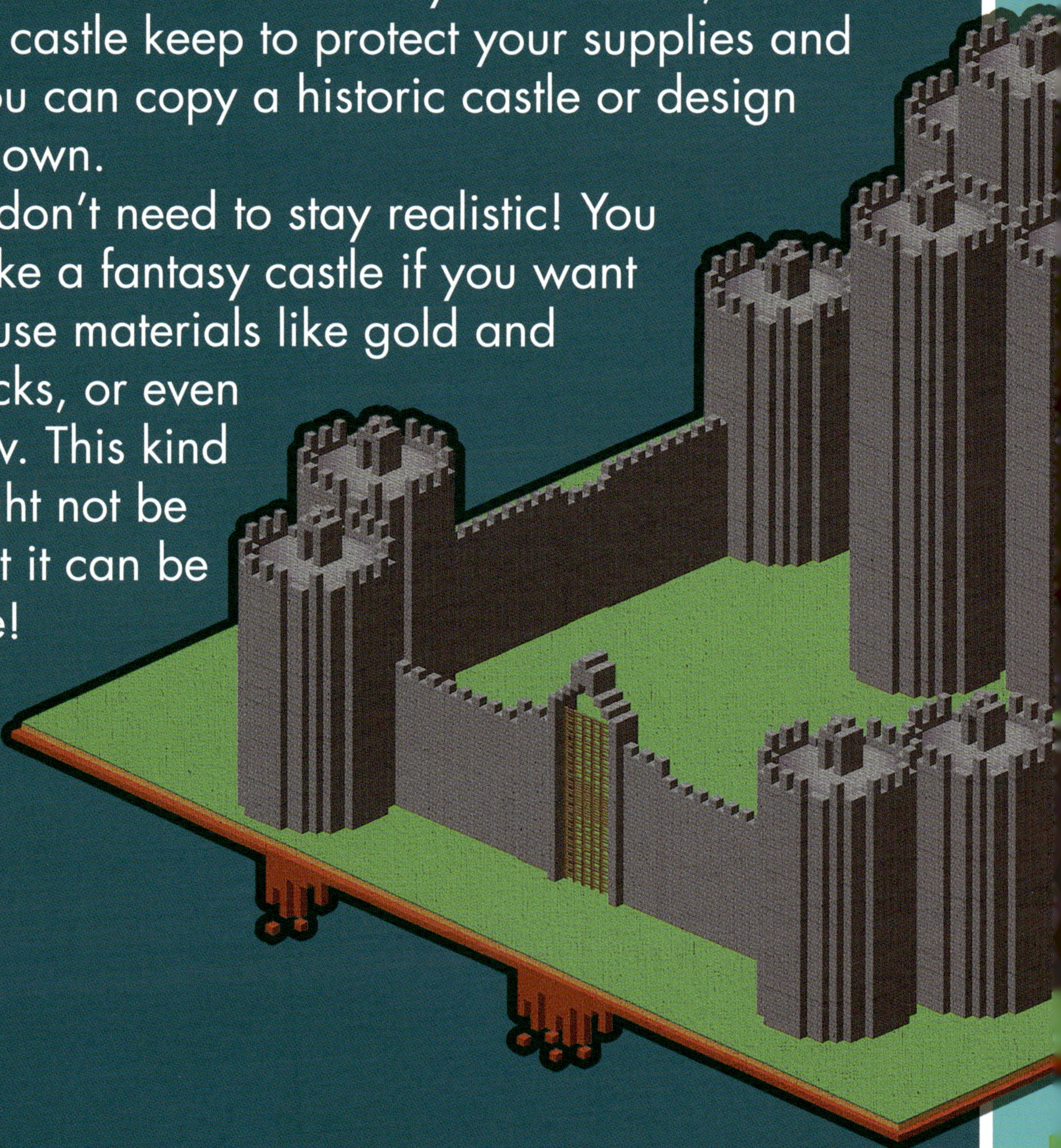

What interesting details can you add to your castle? What about a secret treasure room or hidden passages?

GLOSSARY

creative Showing an ability to think of new things or ideas.
defense A way of guarding against an enemy.
design To create the pattern or shape of something. Also, the pattern or shape of something.
detail A small part of something.
explosion A sudden release of energy.
flexibility The ability to bend or change easily.
fortify To add material to strengthen or improve.
gravity The force that pulls objects toward the center of a planet or star. The force that pulls objects toward Earth's center.
material Matter from which something is made.
protective Keeping safe.
siege The presence of an army around a place to try to force its people to give up.
spawn In a video game, to appear or cause something to appear.

FOR MORE INFORMATION

BOOKS

Future Publishing. *Cool Builds in Minecraft.* New York, NY: Scholastic Inc., 2018.
Mojang AB. *Minecraft: Exploded Builds: Medieval Fortress.* New York, NY: Del Rey, 2017.
National Geographic Kids. *Knights and Castles Sticker Activity Book.* Washington, DC: National Geographic Kids, 2020.

WEBSITES

Minecraft Castle Ideas
www.pcgamesn.com/minecraft/castle-ideas-blueprints
Learn how to use blueprints to build different *Minecraft* castles.

15 Best Minecraft Castles
codakid.com/minecraft-castles/
This guide offers tutorials and examples of different *Minecraft* castle builds.

The Best Minecraft Castle Ideas
www.pcgamer.com/best-minecraft-castle-ideas-building-blueprints-designs/
Visit *Minecraft* castle builds through this site.

Publisher's note to educators and parents: Our editors have carefully reviewed these websites to ensure that they are suitable for students. Many websites change frequently, however, and we cannot guarantee that a site's future contents will continue to meet our high standards of quality and educational value. Be advised that students should be closely supervised whenever they access the internet.

INDEX